This Book Belongs To:

....

BE STRONG, and let your HEART, take courage, all you who wait for the LORD

PSALM 31:24

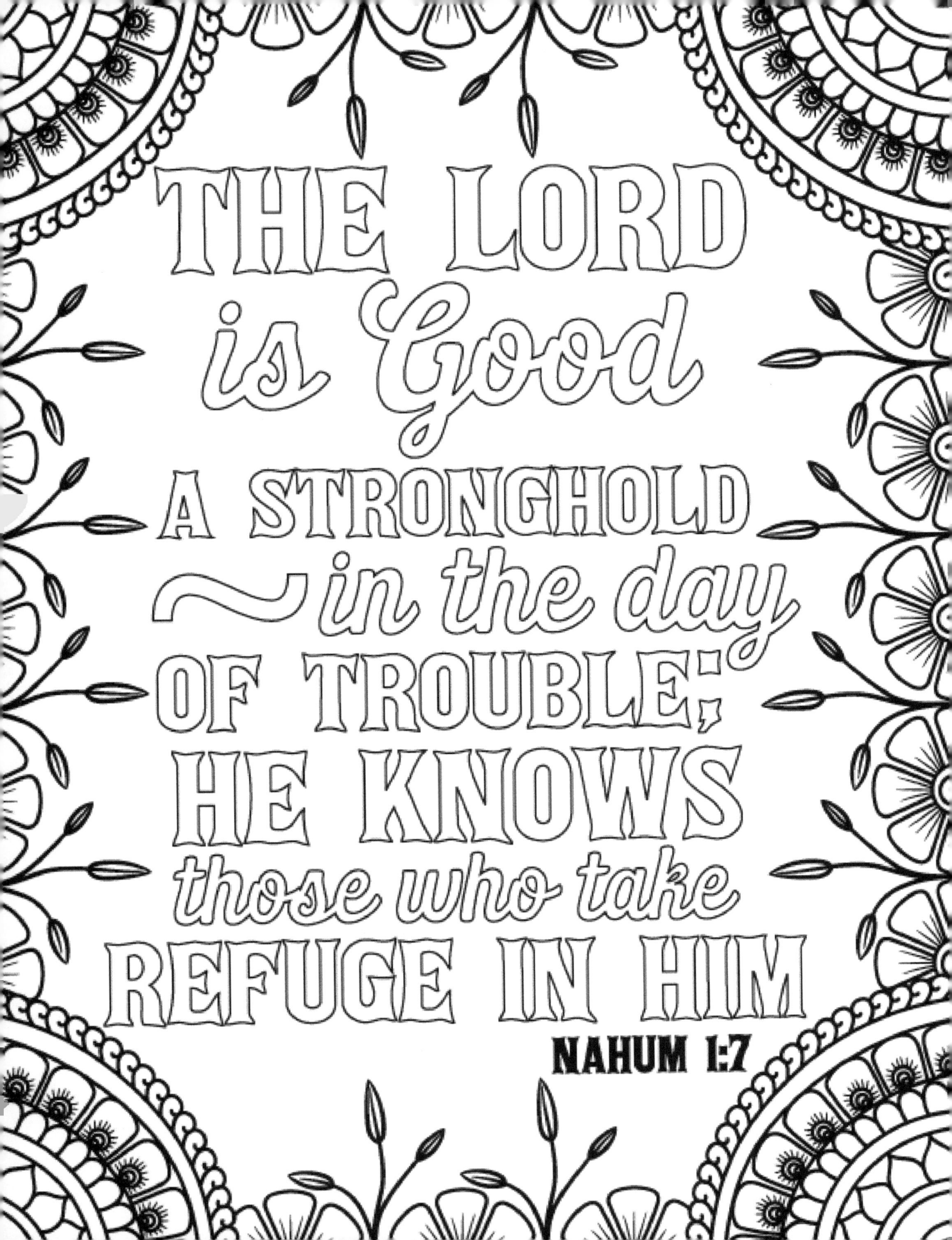

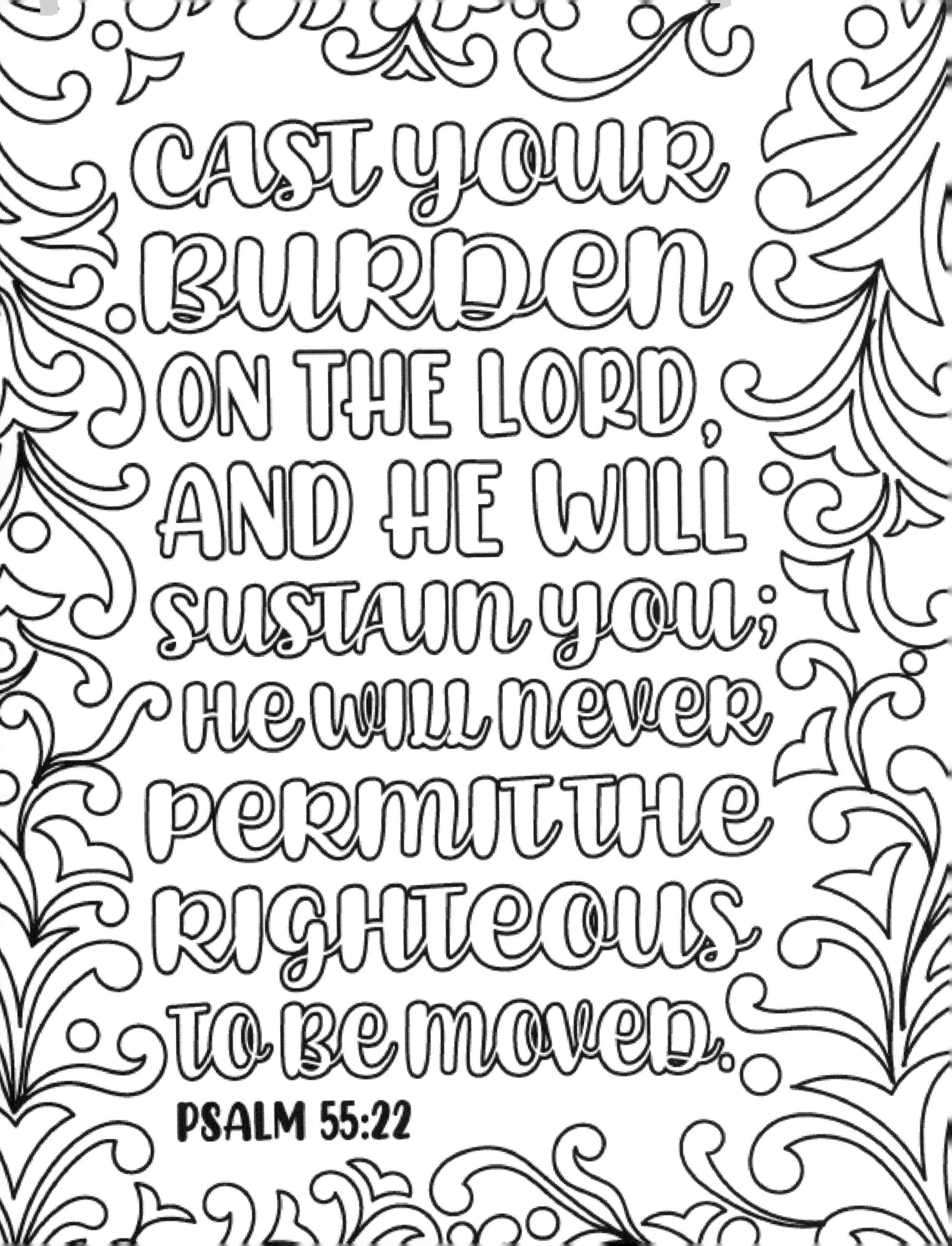

CAST YOUR BURDEN ON THE LORD, AND HE WILL SUSTAIN YOU; HE WILL NEVER PERMIT THE RIGHTEOUS TO BE MOVED.

PSALM 55:22

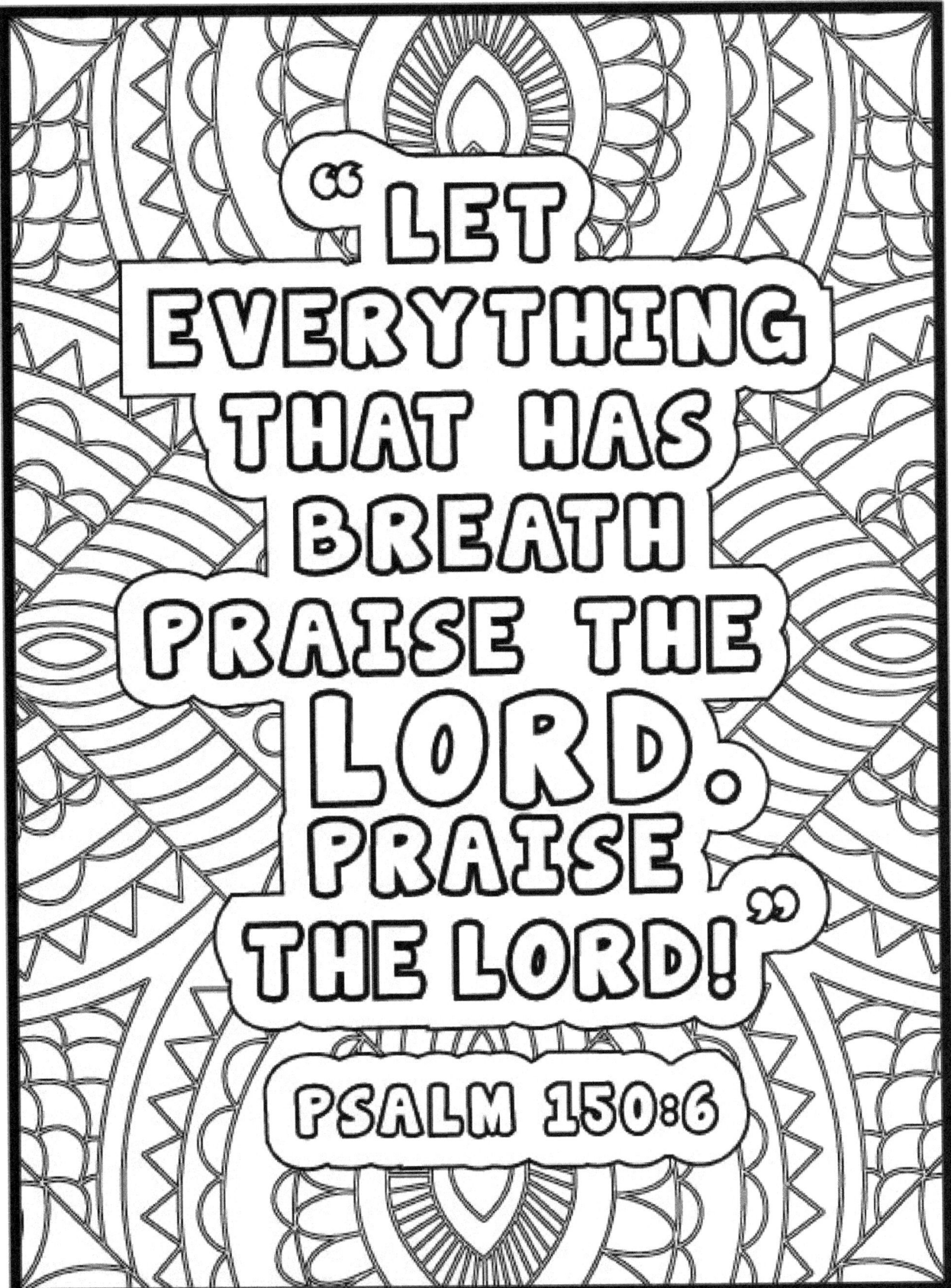

THE WORD
of the
LORD
STANDS
FOREVER
[ISAIAH 40:8]

Psalms 23:1

Whenever I fear I will trust in You.

Psalm 56:3

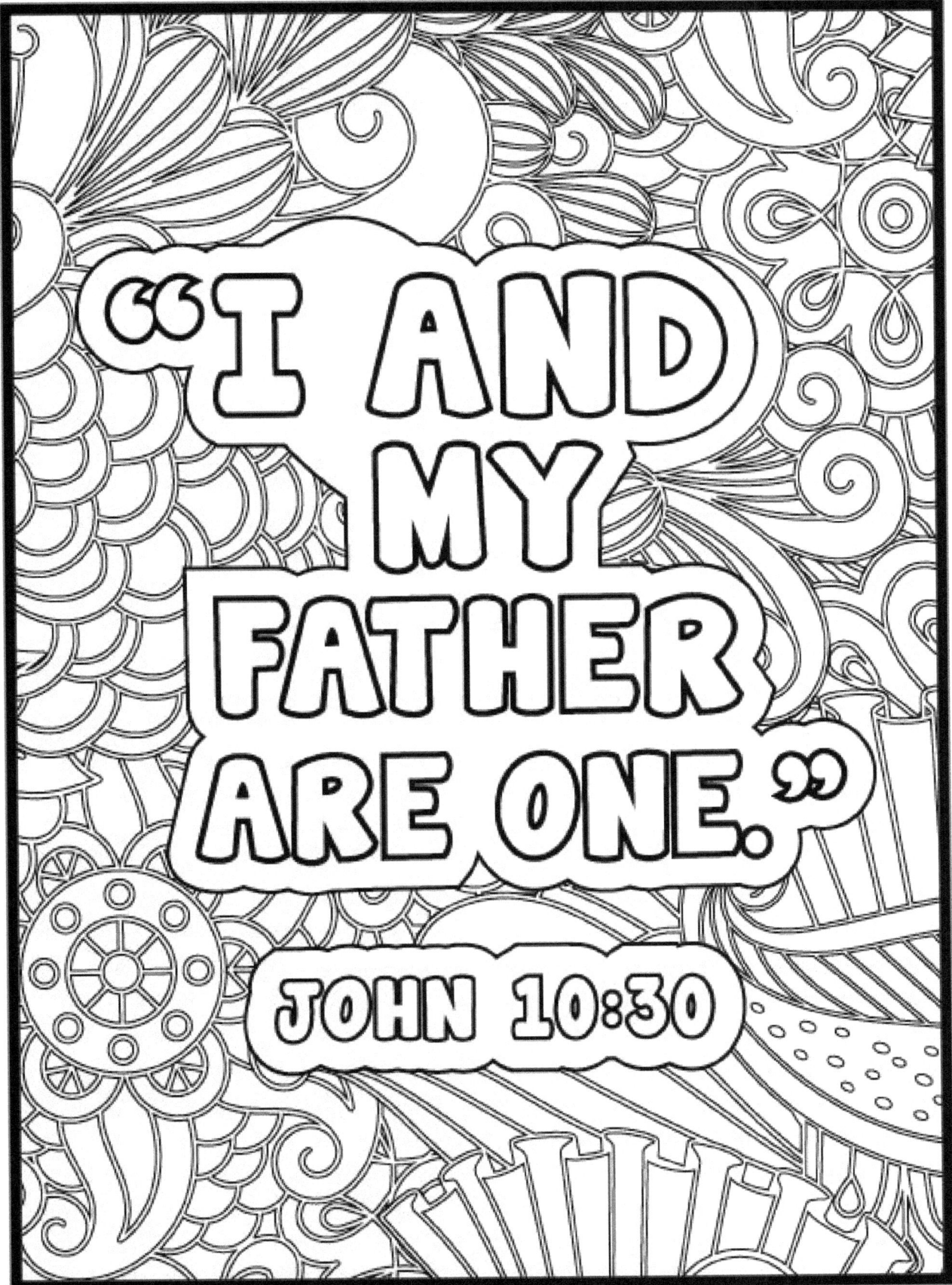

ON THE DAY I CALLED, YOU ANSWERED ME: MY STRENGTH OF SOUL YOU INCREASED

PSALM 138:3

Psalm 118:6

When the RIGHTEOUS cry for help THE LORD hears and DELIVERS THEM OUT OF ALL THEIR troubles

(PSALM 34:17)

This is my COMFORT in my AFFLICTION THAT YOUR Promise gives me Life

Psalm 119:50

HE ONLY is my Rock AND MY Salvation, MY FORTRESS: I SHALL NOT BE Shaken

PSALM 62:6

Come
TO ME
ALL WHO LABOR
And are
HEAVY LADEN
AND I WILL
GIVE YOU
Rest
MATTHEW 11:28

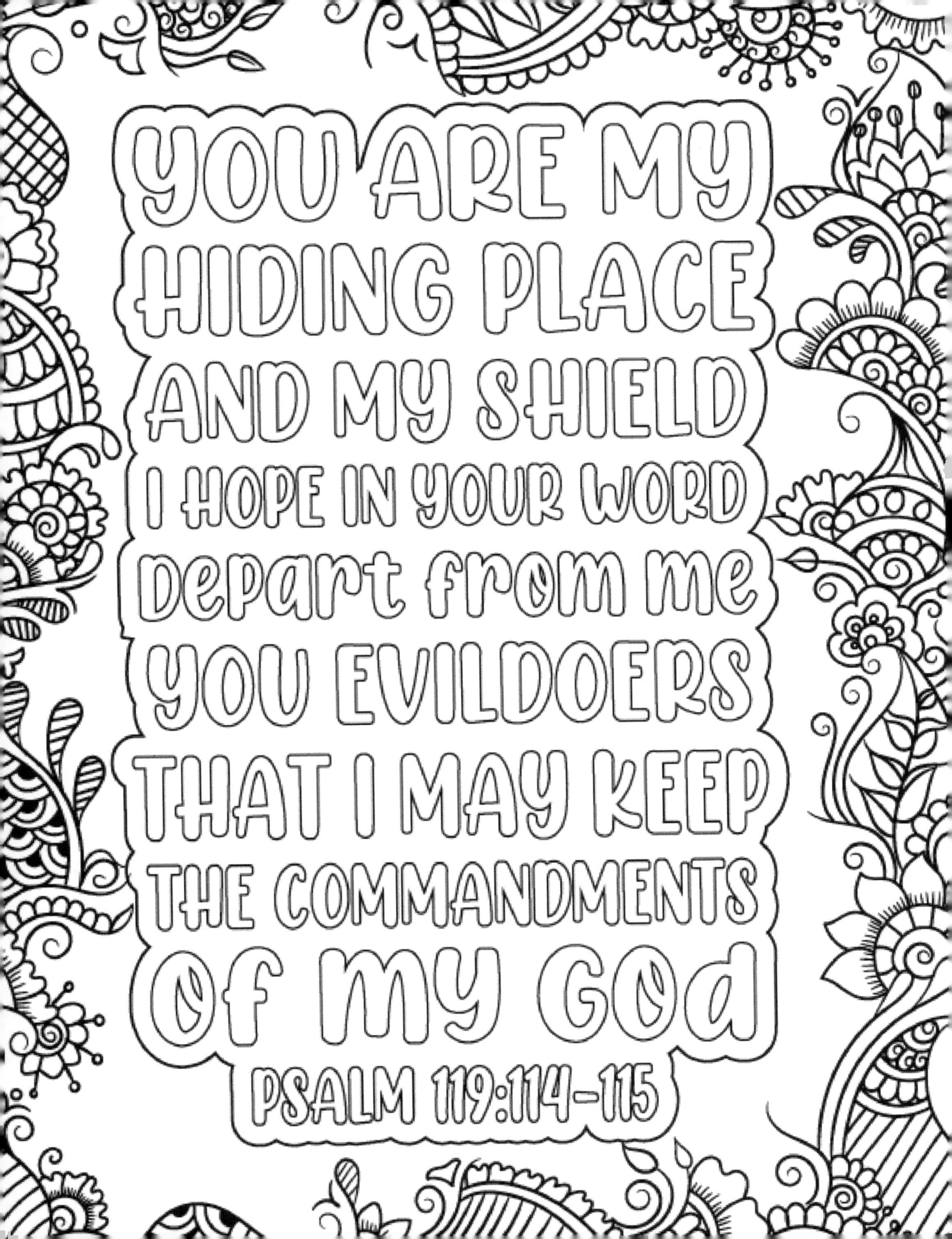

YOU ARE MY HIDING PLACE AND MY SHIELD I HOPE IN YOUR WORD DEPART FROM ME YOU EVILDOERS THAT I MAY KEEP THE COMMANDMENTS OF MY GOD

PSALM 119:114-115

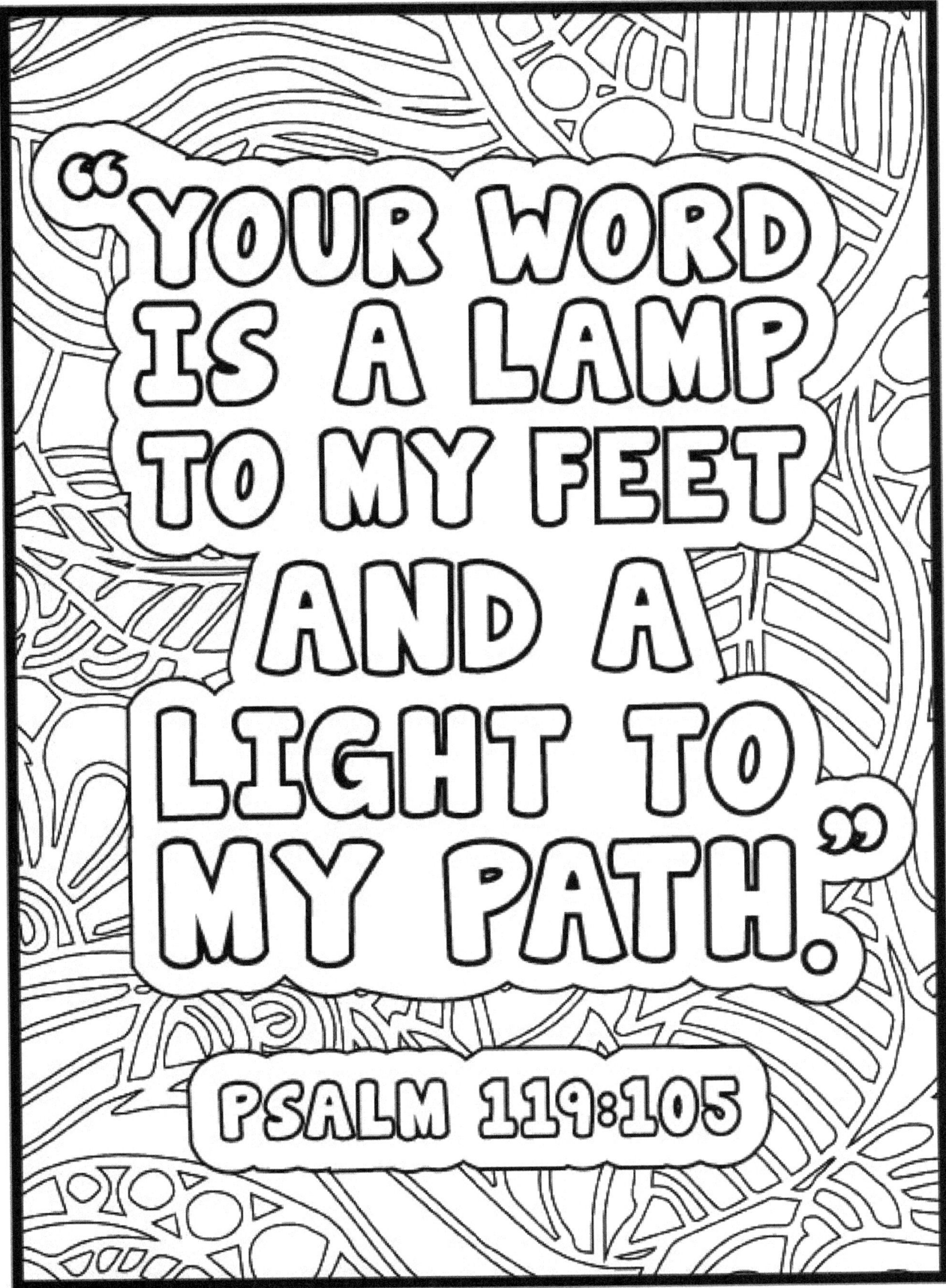

God Will Command His Angels To Protect You Wherever You Go.

Psalm 91:11

Psalm 27:4

THE LORD IS MY LIGHT AND MY SALVATION; WHOM SHALL I FEAR? THE LORD IS THE STRONGHOLD OF MY LIFE; OF WHOM SHALL I BE AFRAID? PSALM 27:1

I Will Not Fear The Lord Is With Me

Psalm 118:6

Psalms 30:2

O LORD my GOD I cried to You for help and You have healed me.

PRAISE THE LORD! FOR GREAT IS HIS LOVE TOWARDS US.

Psalm 117

Psalm 31:24

Be strong and take heart, all you who hope in the Lord.

WHEN I AM AFRAID, I PUT MY TRUST IN YOU. IN GOD, WHOSE WORD I PRAISE—IN GOD I TRUST AND AM NOT AFRAID.

Psalm 56:3

I love you, Lord, my strength.

Psalm 18:1

It is God who arms me with strength and keeps my way secure.

Psalm 18:32

Psalm 9:9

The Lord is a refuge for the oppressed, a stronghold in times of trouble.

Psalm 25:1

In you, Lord my God, I put my trust.

Be strong and take heart, all you who hope in the Lord.

Psalm 31:24

LORD, our Lord, how majestic is your name in all the earth!

Psalms 8

THY word is a lamp for my feet, a light on my path.

Psalms 119:105